GUILT AND GINGERBREAD

Leon Garfield

GUILT
AND
GINGERBREAD

Illustrated by Fritz Wegner

VIKING KESTREL

VIKING KESTREL

Penguin Books, Harmondsworth, Middlesex, England

Viking Penguin Inc., 40 West 23rd Street, New York, New York 10010, U.S.A.

Penguin Books Australia Ltd, Ringwood, Victoria, Australia

Penguin Books Canada Ltd, 2801 John Street, Markham, Ontario, Canada L3R 1B4

Penguin Books (N.Z.) Ltd, 182–190 Wairau Road, Auckland 10, New Zealand

First published in 1984

British Library Cataloguing in Publication Data

Garfield, Leon
Guilt and gingerbread
I. Title
823'.914[J]   PZ7

ISBN 0–670–80012–0

Printed in Great Britain by
Richard Clay (The Chaucer Press) Ltd,
Bungay, Suffolk

For my daughter, Jane

ONE

It's a fact that travel broadens the mind; and it's a fact that, if you do it on a horse, it broadens the bottom, too. That was why Giorgio walked almost as much as he rode, for his good looks were all he had in the world to bless himself with.

'There goes a merciful young man!' people exclaimed, as he trudged through village and hamlet on his way to the River Rhine. 'For see how merciful he is to his beast!'

Gladly they gave him food and shelter, and oats for his melancholy bag of bones; and, when he set off again, they wished him luck.

He was a poor student of philosophy from Padua University, whose night-long studies in a dusty attic had revealed to him no more than that it was better to be rich than poor; and that, unless he made haste and found himself a rich wife while he still had the good looks to catch one, he would end up as frayed and thin and smelly as his wise professors.

So early one morning, he'd packed up his possessions, kissed his landlady good-bye, and set off for the castle of Oberweselberg, and the Princess Charlotte, whose fame had spread even to Padua.

She ruled, so they said, not with a rod of iron, but with a heart of gold. Nobody was ever turned away from her doors; and the only ones who left with long faces were suitors, who came in droves from far and wide to seek her hand in marriage.

She would have none of them. The rich, the famous and the nobly born all met with the same fate. She'd listen to them politely, thank them for the honour of their attentions; and gently shake her head. Then, when they'd gone away, she'd distribute the rich gifts they'd brought her among the people of her little town by the River Rhine; and when she lay in her bed at night, she'd sigh:

> 'Heart of gold, heart of gold,
> Must be given, never sold.'

It would have been a precious gift indeed; and people said that whoever won it would be gaining a treasure beyond compare.

'– To say nothing,' estimated Giorgio, who had looked up Oberweselberg in a gazetteer, 'of a noble residence in the Baroque style, with two hundred rooms, four hundred acres of ornamental gardens and woodland, containing many unusual trees, and a town with three breweries, many first-class inns serving local dishes, and a thriving trade on the River Rhine.'

It was springtime when Giorgio crossed the mountains, and high summer when at last he reached the valley of the Rhine. The days were full of sunshine and sharp shadows, and butterflies fragile as thoughts. As he walked and rode, walked and rode, along the winding dusty by-ways and lanes, he conversed with the ancient companion of his journey; for there was none else by.

'Do you think,' he asked his horse, as doubts began to enter his mind, 'that she's already married, and I'll be too late?'

'Na-ay!' answered the animal, shaking its head and rattling its brains with a noise like loose harness. 'Na-ay!'

'Do you not think,' pursued Giorgio, 'that I am aiming too high; and that a princess would not look twice upon a poor student of philosophy, no matter how far he has come?'

'Na-ay!' responded the sagacious creature, without a moment's delay.

'Then you don't think,' asked Giorgio earnestly, 'that my landlady was right when she warned me that I'd get no more than supper and a bed for the night, and I'd be better off in Padua, and paying the rent?'

'Na-ay!' the horse assured him; and Giorgio sighed with relief.

'There's a good fellow!' he said, patting his companion on the nose before climbing up on his back. 'Forward!' he cried, digging in his heels. 'Forward to Princess Charlotte and her heart of gold!'

'NA-AY!' screamed the horse. 'NA-AY! NA-AY!' and it shied in panic as they rounded a bend in the road.

There was an old woman by the side of the road. She was sitting contentedly in a broken-down armchair, as if the world was her parlour and the sun her fireside. She was busily sewing, with a needle that flashed and shimmered, as fast as a dragon-fly's wing.

'Good morning, young sir!' she croaked, scarcely troubling to look up from her work.

'Good morning to you, mother,' returned Giorgio, sliding down off his horse for a closer look at what the old woman was making.

He marvelled to see her wrinkled fingers move so quick that

at times she seemed to be stitching without either needle or thread. Presently she stopped; and, with a pair of scissors that darted like a silver kingfisher, she snipped through a spider-fine length of red silk. Then she looked up; and her face was as pecked and wrinkled as an old apple.

'I know just what's in your mind, young sir,' she said.

'Do you now!' said Giorgio in surprise. 'What do you suppose is in my mind?'

'This!' answered she, holding up her sewing in front of her face, as if to hide a sudden wolfish glitter that had come into her eyes. 'You were thinking what a fine present it would make for our Princess Charlotte!'

It was a bride veil; and, even if you knew nothing about sewing, you could see that it was a wonder of workmanship. It was as fine as a cobweb, and was embroidered all over with red roses that were so real that they seemed to fill the air with their perfume.

'True enough,' admitted Giorgio, staring at the veil. 'The thought had crossed my mind.'

'And what did it find when it got to the other side?' demanded the old woman keenly, putting aside the veil and folding her hands in her lap.

Giorgio did not choose to answer.

'Then I'll tell you what it found,' she informed him. 'It found that you don't have enough money to pay me for it.'

'You don't need to be a fortune-teller to have guessed that!' said the poor student of philosophy, with a rueful smile.

'I don't tell fortunes, young sir! It's against the law. I make them instead.' Suddenly she smiled a smile of a million wrinkles. 'And I know what's in your mind right now,' she chuckled. 'You're thinking, how come, if she can make fortunes, that she's sitting in a raggedy old chair, doing needlework by the side of the road!'

'The thought,' granted Giorgio, 'had crossed my mind, mother.'

'And I won't inquire,' said she coolly, 'how short a journey that was!'

Giorgio looked offended, so she went on more humbly: 'To be honest with you, young sir, I sit here sewing, like a poor old woman, because what I want cannot be bought with money. And yet money must buy it.'

'I don't follow you, mother,' said Giorgio, puzzled.

'You can if you will,' said she, creaking to her feet and hobbling towards the trees that stood back from the road. 'Follow me, I mean.' She beckoned to him and called out: 'Bring my chair, if you would be so kind. It might rain.'

The chair proved heavy and awkward; and his horse watched with fond sympathy as he staggered under its weight and blundered after the old woman. There was no doubt that she had succeeded in fascinating him; not with her looks, of course, but by her interesting words about money.

She led him to her home, which stood quaintly in a clearing; but this was only for the time being, she made haste to explain, until she found somewhere more convenient, with running water and nearer to the shops.

It was a caravan or, more properly, a cottage on wheels. It was painted white with brown stripes, in the Tudor style; and looked like a cake, of the variety that pastry-cooks call Fancies.

Giorgio put down the chair but, before he could say a word, the old woman raised a warning finger.

'Hold your tongue, young sir,' she muttered mysteriously. 'Corn has ears, you know, and potatoes have eyes, and mice carry tales!'

He laughed; but nevertheless did as he was told. He waited, while the old woman climbed up the two wooden steps to her front door and disappeared into her house, like a bulky grey moth, folding. There were sounds of curtains being drawn and crockery being cleared away; and then the old woman's face appeared at a window, nodding and smiling, and inviting him into her sitting-room.

It was like anybody else's sitting-room, inasmuch as there seemed nowhere to sit down without knocking something over. There were little tables and shelves, all elbow-high, crowded with china ornaments and hundreds and hundreds of reels of coloured silk thread, that kept falling on the floor and scuttling eagerly into corners, so that Giorgio was forever banging his head against furniture in his efforts to catch them and put them back. And there were dozens of photographs in frames that looked as if they were made of silver toothpaste, squeezed out.

Mostly they were of royalty, waving from balconies, congratulating horses, or just standing bolt upright and decorated like Christmas trees. Giorgio was undeniably impressed.

'There's a beautiful girl!' he exclaimed, pointing to a picture

that seemed to occupy pride of place. It was of a singularly
lovely young woman, smiling out of a pale brown fog, and
wearing pearls. 'Could that be the Princess Charlotte,
mother?'

'It could be,' she said, 'but it isn't. It's me, when I was
eighteen. There's our princess.' She nodded towards a framed
bank-note that hung upon the wall. The Princess was depicted
in profile, gazing serenely at Oberweselberg, and either five or
fifty thousand marks, there being more noughts than Giorgio
was used to. She was the most beautiful creature Giorgio had
ever seen; and he wondered how many lire there were to the
Oberweselberg mark.

'As you can see,' said the old woman, 'I live very simply, and surrounded by my memories. I have everything I need; but I don't have the one thing that I want.'

'And what might that be, mother?' inquired Giorgio, politely transferring his gaze from the bank-note to the old woman.

'It might be anything, young sir,' she said, 'but it isn't. What I want is Princess Charlotte's golden heart.'

'I – I beg your pardon!' stammered Giorgio, wondering if his hearing had been damaged by his head having been banged against the furniture so many times. 'I didn't quite catch what you said!'

'Then you should have listened with your ears, young sir, and not with your hands. I said that I wanted the princess's golden heart.'

'Ah!' said Giorgio, thinking it was high time he was going, and knocking down a reel of pink silk that ran away under a table to play with its friends. 'Now I see what you meant when you said that money couldn't buy it, mother!'

'Ah! But have you forgotten that I said that money *must* buy it?'

'Come now, mother,' said Giorgio, sensibly, 'how can you buy something like Princess Charlotte's golden heart?'

'If there was something like it, young sir, I would not want it.'

'True, true. Then how do you propose to buy it, mother?'

'By buying you, young sir.'

'And what good would that do you, mother?' asked Giorgio, surprised into a modesty he didn't really mean.

'I will buy you with a fine mansion, gardens and woods, a little town; and a beautiful wife. I will make sure that you gain the Princess Charlotte. And, in return, you will bring me her golden heart.'

'How? Would you have me murder her?' asked Giorgio, mightily alarmed, and wondering how best he might make his escape and fetch the police. 'Would you have me cut her up, like the cats' meat man?'

'Come,' said she. 'Give me your hand.'

He held it out, thinking that she was going to read his fortune in his palm. But no such thing. She seized his wrist and, with one huge snip of her kingfisher scissors, laid his arm wide open, sleeve and flesh, right down to the pale, astonished bone!

He shrieked aloud when he saw what had happened; but it was in terror rather than in pain. He hadn't felt so much as the scissors' prick.

'I'll die, mother!' he howled. 'I'll bleed to death!'

'Keep still, young sir, keep still,' she said calmly. 'What I've undone, I can do up again.'

He shook and trembled, and reflected that no morning in all his life had ended up so badly, while the old woman matched his skin to a reel of silk, threaded her needle, and began to stitch.

He felt no more of the needle than he'd felt of the scissors; and, as he watched with bulging eyes, he saw the great wound begin to disappear as the crooked fingers darted to and fro. Soon she had finished, and she snipped off the end of the thread. Fearfully he examined his arm. It was as good as new; or, rather, as good as it had been before. Nothing showed. Even the end of the thread had vanished. All that remained to betray what had happened was a single spot of blood. And, of course, his damaged sleeve.

'And – and can you mend this, too, mother?' asked Giorgio, shakily.

'Pooh!' said she, contemptuously. 'That's work for a wife!'

Giorgio nodded. He was absolutely no match for the old woman; and his studies had told him that, when you met somebody like that, it was wisest to wait and see. So he sat perfectly still, clutching his ruined sleeve, while the old woman explained to him exactly what he was to do. When she had concluded, she gave him a small leather case in which she had put her scissors, her needle, and a reel of creamy-white thread that was faintly flushed with pink.

'It's a good match,' she said. 'I can promise you that.'

He took it; and then, with a smile, she handed him a black velvet bag.

'For her heart, young sir. For the golden heart.'

'But – but there's something inside.'

'Of course there is. When you take out the heart of gold, you must put something back in its place. Otherwise our princess would die.'

He peered into the bag, and exclaimed in astonishment. Within, in a nest of oiled black silk, lay a heart. But it was a heart fashioned in the finest china, and delicately coloured rose-red.

'A pretty china heart for a pretty china doll!' said the old woman, with a mocking grin. 'Just the wife for a fine-looking young sir like you! But take good care of it. Don't break it. We wouldn't want you to break our princess's heart!'

Then she gave him the bride veil, done up in a brown paper parcel.

'Remember, young sir, exactly what I have told you.'

Giorgio nodded; he was not likely to forget. Then the old woman opened her front door, and Giorgio was surprised to see that the sun was still shining outside, as if nothing had happened. He went down the two wooden steps, scarcely able to support himself on his trembling legs. He felt as if he was already half-way to being a murderer.

'Bring me back the golden heart, young sir,' pleaded the old woman, laying a hand upon his shoulder. Then her voice hardened, and there were glints of menace in it. 'I will be waiting for you,' she said.

The castle of Oberweselberg, standing on top of a hill above the town, looked exactly as it did on the stamps; so much so, that you half-expected to see Twenty Pfennigs engraved on a cloud.

'I won't do it!' thought the poor student, as he toiled up the long, winding hill, with his horse trudging after. 'I'm not a monster, am I!'

'Na-ay!' his horse assured him, with a rattle of its bony head.

The castle was approached through imposing wrought-iron gates, beyond which stretched the celebrated ornamental gardens, which had been laid out in the previous century by the King of France's gardener at a cost of one million francs, and looked like an impossible problem in green geometry.

'It would be better to stay poor and end up as a professor at Padua University,' muttered Giorgio, 'than to have such a crime on my conscience. Do you not think so?'

'Na-ay!' answered the horse; and Giorgio frowned.

Everywhere you looked there were marble fountains, executed by the best Italian masters, hurling silvery necklaces of water high in the air; and bright peacocks strutted across the lawns. Giorgio, fearing that his horse would take fright and throw him, thought it safest to continue walking.

'There goes a merciful young man,' said a gardener to his

boy, who laboured under a heavy pot, 'for see how merciful he is to his beast.'

The castle's noble portico was supported on the heads of four huge maidens, who bore their heavy burden with patient stony smiles.

'It would need a heart like yours,' whispered Giorgio, 'to do what the old woman wants. Do you not think so?'

But before either they or his horse could reply, two servants in blue livery came out to greet him, and a stableboy came running to look after his horse.

It was the princess's custom for all who came to her door, no matter how poor, to be treated with the same courtesy that would be offered to a prince. They were brought directly to see her, so that she herself might inquire into their needs.

Naturally her servants did what they could to protect so kind a mistress against those who came to take advantage, and they always looked carefully at the needier visitor.

'They've guessed!' thought Giorgio in terror, as the servants glanced curiously at his brown paper parcel and the bulging satchel that hung from his shoulder. 'They've guessed what's inside!'

'Na-ay!' reassured his horse as it was led away; and Giorgio sighed with relief.

He was conducted across the famous circular hall and through several splendid apartments, containing, he re-collected, though he did not particularly notice them, several items of valuable porcelain and a four-hundred-piece dinner service presented by the Elector of Hanover, which was reputed to have cost fifty thousand thalers.

'I'll pay my respects to the princess, and nothing else,' decided Giorgio. 'The old woman and her horrible plan can go to the devil where they belong!'

He was taken into a white and gold ante-chamber in which a courtly-looking gentleman was sitting at a desk. The gentle-man smiled at him; and, of course, his eyes went unfailingly to the bulging satchel! Then he asked Giorgio his name, and where he had come from.

'He knows everything!' thought Giorgio, trying to stop the violent knocking of his knees. 'He knows that I've come from the old woman's caravan!' and he shuddered to think that, if this was how he felt *before* he committed the crime, how much worse it would be *afterwards*! 'I'll leave at once! I won't be tempted any more! I won't even look at the princess!'

'Come this way, Signor Giorgio,' said the courtly gentle-man, after the poor student had answered his questions. 'Her Highness will be most interested to hear all about the University of Padua. She has quite a soft spot in her heart for students; particularly of philosophy.'

He rose to his feet and opened a door; and Giorgio, almost fainting under his burden of guilt, was ushered into the presence of the princess.

Her Serene Highness, the Princess Charlotte of Oberweselberg (God bless her and send her a worthy man!), was twenty-one, but did not look an hour more than nineteen. With her golden hair and wide blue eyes, she was the poet's dream and

the painter's despair. In every parlour in Oberweselberg there hung a framed verse in her honour, and a framed picture of her wearing the Order of St Michael and St George; but neither words nor brush could hope to capture the gentle radiance of her presence.

It's said that some people are too beautiful for their own good; but she was too good for her own beauty, and behaved almost as if she was plain. She took no pride in the splendour of her looks, but only in the treasure of her golden heart which, like no other treasure in the world, increased with the spending.

As soon as she saw how pale and frightened the poor student looked – so frightened that he dared not raise his eyes to look at her – she dismissed her secretary and did everything she could to put him at his ease.

Her tenderest feelings were aroused. She begged the student to sit down and compose himself. She wasn't an ogre, she promised him, she wasn't going to eat him; and, with her own hands, she poured him out a glass of Oberweselberg wine and offered to relieve him of the satchel that seemed to be weighing him down.

'No, no!' cried Giorgio, in utter terror. 'You must not do that, Your Highness! Please –'

'Very well, Signor Giorgio,' said she. 'But I beg of you, try to be calm, or else we shall never become acquainted.'

Little by little Giorgio recovered, and reflected that, as he was not going to commit the crime, he ought to stop worrying about it.

'That's better, Signor Giorgio,' said the princess. 'For a moment I feared that you were going to run away from me!'

'The thought,' admitted Giorgio, 'had crossed my mind, Your Highness.'

'Then I'm glad it didn't linger,' she said, with a strange smile; and went on to question him about his studies, and to ask him why he had left his dusty attic in Padua.

'For a quest, Your Highness,' answered Giorgio promptly; and then he remembered, with a chill of dread, that that was what the old woman had told him to say. 'She will ask you why you left Padua; and you will answer: "For a quest, Your Highness." Then she will ask you, "Was it a quest for a fortune, or for a bride?" '

22

'And was it, Signor Giorgio,' inquired the princess, 'a quest for a fortune, or for a bride?'

He shook: he trembled; his brain began to spin.

'My bride will be my fortune,' he responded helplessly. 'She will bring me the fortune of her heart.'

'Spoken like a true philosopher, Signor Giorgio. And what will you bring to her?'

'This, Your Highness!' answered Giorgio, feeling more like a fly caught in a terrible web than a true philosopher. He opened the brown paper parcel and shook out the marvellous bride veil. 'It was given to me by a saintly old woman on the one condition that I would give it only to the bride who was worthy of it.'

'And is that why you have come to Oberweselberg?' asked the princess, fascinated by the wondrous workmanship of the veil.

Giorgio said nothing. The old woman had warned to say nothing, and to let the question hover unanswered in the air.

She frowned slightly; and summoned her secretary to take the poor student to a room where he might rest for the night. He looked so pale, she said, and weary from his travels. She would be pleased to see him at dinner . . .

'I will stay just for this one night,' thought Giorgio, who had been meaning to leave directly. 'There can't be any harm in that, because I will not commit the crime. No! Not for all the fine porcelain and ornamental gardens in the world! Good heavens! What did the old woman take me for!'

Dinner was served in the great dining-room, where gentlemen as smart as magpies, and ladies all fringed and beaded, like lampshades, sat down at a table as long as a street. The poor student, with a countess on one side, and a Minister of State on the other, was much divided between trying to keep his torn sleeve out of his soup, and admiring the crystal chandeliers, the silver knives and forks, and the entrancing beauty of the princess.

'I'm glad I stayed to see all this,' thought Giorgio, 'because it shows what a fine character I have to resist the old woman's temptation.'

The princess hardly addressed a word to him until dinner was over and she was about to leave the room.

'Tomorrow morning, Signor Giorgio,' she said, 'you must go down into the town. Perhaps it will be among the young ladies of Oberweselberg that you will find the object of your quest.'

'Tomorrow morning,' thought Giorgio, 'I will be off and away for ever!' But of course he said nothing of his intention, because it would have seemed like a slight upon the people of her town.

When morning came, his horse was brought round to the castle's entrance. It was groomed and shining, as it had never shone before. Its harness was tightened, so that its brains no longer rattled and, all in all, it looked so brisk and mettlesome, that Giorgio wondered if it was safe to mount up on its back; but the worthy creature bore him uncomplainingly all the way down into the town.

Oberweselberg was, exactly as the gazetteer said, a pretty little town of ten thousand inhabitants. Its quaint streets and picturesque houses, with their brightly painted shutters, might have come straight from the pages of a fairy-tale; while, at the same time, it possessed up-to-date sanitation and an excellent public transport system. The principal inns were situated around the fine old market square, in the middle of which stood the famous stone cross of St Wesel, and a fountain which, once a year, on St Wesel's Day (August 23rd) flowed with Oberweselberg beer. Early closing on Thursdays.

'It would be no small thing to be prince of such a town,' murmured Giorgio, gazing about him. 'But unfortunately I have too noble a nature to commit a crime for it. Come, old companion,' he said to his horse. 'Shall we go back to Padua?'

'Na-ay!' answered the animal, staring thirstily at a horse-trough that stood by the fountain. 'Na-ay!'

On the side of the trough was engraved the sentiment: 'A
merciful man is merciful to his beast.' Giorgio gazed at his
horse which, after only one night in the castle's stables, looked
twenty years younger. Would it be merciful, he wondered, to
drive the poor creature all the way back over the mountains

without giving it the benefit of just one more night of care and
comfort?

'Na–ay!' said the horse; and Giorgio felt that, for the animal's
sake, he must expose his own nobility to yet another night of
trial.

'And did you,' asked the princess, when he returned to the
castle, 'find the object of your quest among the young ladies of
the town?'

For answer, Giorgio showed her the brown paper parcel,
and shook his head.

'Then you must try again tomorrow,' she said; and gave
him so warm a smile that it remained in his mind all day, and
took away his appetite, so that he scarcely touched a crumb of
his dinner.

It haunted him as he lay in his bed that night, and he wondered, over and over again, what it meant. Could she have fallen in love with him, exactly as the old woman had promised she would? His heart beat fast as prospects of greatness filled his brain. He tried to put them from him, but the more he thought about the princess's smile, the more he felt sure that she had fallen in love with him.

He became terribly frightened. 'It just shows,' he whispered to himself, 'how easy it is to be caught in a situation you have done your best to avoid! But thank heavens that I've seen the danger in time!'

He got out of bed and went to the window to examine his watch. It was three o'clock in the morning. Quickly he dressed himself. He would creep away while the castle was asleep. Then he would go back to the old woman and return her horrible gifts, and tell her to her face that he, like the princess's golden heart, was not to be bought with money.

He slung the bulging satchel over his shoulder, and, with the parcel under his arm, left the room and tiptoed down the stairs.

'When you reach the next floor down,' the old woman had said, 'turn left, go along the passage until you come to a corner. Then turn right and go to the end. There you will find a door with a golden crown above it. It is the door to the princess's bedroom.'

'Very well,' muttered Giorgio. 'I will go there, just to show you that I have the strength not to go inside.'

He reached the floor below. He turned left. He went along the passage until he came to a corner. He turned right; and there, at the end, dimly gleaming in the starlight that crept through a window, he saw the door with the golden crown above it. He moved towards it; but so quietly that none could have told which was Giorgio and which was his shadow. He stood outside the door.

'To stay here, and then to creep away,' breathed Giorgio, 'would show that I was frightened to trust myself. But if I went inside, only for a moment, of course! and stood alone with the princess before I went away, it would show, once and for all, what a fine and steadfast person I really am.'

He opened the door and, pale and noiseless as a ghost, slipped into the princess's bedroom, and shut the door behind him. He stood, quite still. The air was filled with the perfume of roses, and he could hear the princess breathing gently.

She lay in her great four-poster bed, and the starry night shone faintly through the tall windows upon her lovely sleeping face.

'I must draw nearer, I must stand right over her,' whispered Giorgio. 'I must show that, even when everything was within my grasp, I still had the nobility to turn away from the crime.'

He stood over her, and gazed down at the rising and falling of her breast. He put down his satchel, and took out the black velvet bag and the leather case.

'I must hold these things in my hand,' he breathed, 'if I am really to test myself. I must take out the scissors, the needle and thread, and the china heart, exactly as if I was really going to do it. Only then will I be able to say, when I am a frayed old professor in Padua University, that I once had the chance to be rich, but I put honour above worldly gain. Yes, yes! I must thread the needle, I must draw back the sheet, I must hold the scissors, and – and . . . NO!'

But it was too late. The scissors seemed to have leaped in his fingers! Without his ever meaning it, without his ever wanting it, without his ever dreaming it would happen, they had snipped, quick as a kingfisher, through silk, flesh and bone, and laid bare the princess's golden heart!

There it lay, in its shining rosy nest, gleaming and beating . . .

'A – a – a – ah!' sighed the princess. 'A – a – a – ah!'

The poor student gazed down at the huge wound in amazement and terror. He dared not look away. He was a murderer! He felt there were eyes everywhere, staring at him. The very stars accused him; and the air was full of whispers: 'Murderer, murderer!'

Suddenly he remembered what the old woman had said. 'What I have undone, I can do up again.' He began to breathe more easily. Things weren't as bad as they looked. He must sew up the wound and then creep away as if nothing had happened. Because nothing would have happened. As long as he had the power to do up what he had undone, he would not have committed the crime.

In fact, the more you thought about it, the more it showed what an exceptional person he was. If he hadn't gone as close as he had towards committing the crime, nobody could have been sure that he would have had the moral courage to say, 'No! I won't do it!'

And it took courage to stand there, to look down upon the marvellous golden heart, to wonder about it, even to think of touching it –

'A – a – a – ah!' sighed the princess.

How warm it was! One could almost understand why the old woman wanted it so much. It was beautiful, and seemed to glow with its own wondrous life. He wondered what the old woman meant to do with it. She was no fool; she couldn't have wanted it just to keep on her mantelpiece. It must have some extraordinary value for her to have offered him the princess herself in exchange for it.

Giorgio frowned, and began to wonder if he would really be getting the better of the bargain, and not giving away something that was worth a great deal more than what he would be getting. But how could he find out?

Perhaps if he held the heart in his hand . . . only for a moment, of course!

'A – a – a – ah!' sighed the princess.

How heavy it was! It must have weighed more than a pound!

And what a strange sensation its ceaseless throbbing gave him! But he was no nearer to discovering the secret of its value than he had been before.

The poor student shook his head. Nobody, not even the wisest of his professors, could possibly have solved such a mystery in a matter of moments. One would need to study the golden heart for at least a day, if one wanted to learn its true value. One would need to replace it with the china heart . . .

'A – a – a – ah!' sighed the princess, as her golden heart was wrapped up in oiled silk and put into the black velvet bag. She stirred, and murmured faintly in her troubled sleep:

> 'Heart of gold, heart of gold,
> Must be given, never sold.'

She'd woken up! Panic seized Giorgio; and the china heart slipped from his trembling fingers! Before he could catch it, it fell to the floor and smashed into a hundred pieces!

The princess moaned. The colour had gone from her cheeks, and her lips were grey. She was dying!

'When you take out the heart of gold,' the old woman had warned him, 'you must put something in its place. Otherwise our princess will die.'

There was a table by her bed. On it was a yellow apple, almost the size of a heart, and almost the colour of gold. He snatched it up and laid it in the princess's empty breast.

The princess stirred and moaned again. Anxiously he looked at her face. The colour had come back into her cheeks, and her lips were red again! He fancied that she was smiling . . .

He looked at the apple. To his amazement it was covered over, as if an invisible spider had spun a web of vessels and veins!

His panic had been needless; everything was all right. He marvelled at his own presence of mind.

'Giorgio!' murmured the princess in her sleep. 'A – a – ah! Giorgio!'

Deftly he set to work with the needle and thread, which matched the princess as exactly as if it had been made for her. Soon, there was nothing to show for what had happened, beyond a single drop of blood that had fallen on the counterpane, and had dried like an embroidered cherry. Then he gathered up all the pieces of the china heart from the floor, hid them in his satchel, and crept away . . .

As soon as he was back in his room, he concealed the velvet bag in the back of his wardrobe. Then he sat down on his bed and held his head in his hands.

'I am a monster,' he whispered. 'I really am a monster. Don't you think so?'

But his horse was asleep in the castle stables, so there was none to say to him, 'Na–ay!'

He had a horrible dream. He dreamed that he had cut out the princess's heart and had hidden it in a black velvet bag at the back of his wardrobe. It was so real that he was frightened to look inside the wardrobe in case it should turn out to be true. Then he looked, and it *was* true; and he needed all his strength to stop himself rushing outside and shouting to everybody what he had done!

The morning was bright and the sun was everywhere. He could hear servants stirring and going cheerfully about their work. He lay in his bed, with his head under the blanket, waiting for the shriek of dismay that must come when it was discovered what had happened to the princess.

But everything went on as usual. At length he rose and dressed himself and went downstairs. He had a disagreeable feeling that the word 'monster' was painted across his forehead. But nobody seemed to notice. Then he felt it was painted across his back.

Miserably he remembered his own thoughts about how much worse he'd feel *after* he'd committed the crime than he'd felt before. He had been right. He did feel worse. He envied every servant, every member of the princess's household, who could surely have nothing on their consciences to compare with the dreadful burden he carried on his own. What could *they* know of suffering? He grew almost angry with them for looking happy.

He did not dare to ask about the princess; he felt condemned to wait to be told. Then he received a message. The princess

had gone out early; but had left word that Signor Giorgio should again go down into the town to seek the object of his quest.

She was alive! Giorgio could hardly believe his good luck. The worst hadn't happened. He was not a murderer after all!

'And – and how was Her Highness this morning?' he asked the maid who had brought him the message. 'I mean, was she well?'

'Brisk and cheerful, Signor Giorgio,' came the answer. 'Just as usual.'

He was so thankful to hear that she was in good health that he quite forgot, for a moment, why she might not have been. In fact, he honestly believed that his strong feeling of gratitude showed what a generous and warm-hearted nature he had.

He wondered if anything had been said about the missing apple and the spot of blood; but the maid did not mention them. The only notable matter she remarked upon was that Her Highness was limping a little because she had hurt her foot.

Giorgio expressed sympathy, but was not deeply concerned. After all, whatever the princess had done to her foot was no business of his, so he could hardly be expected to grieve over it.

'She cut it,' said the maid, 'on a piece of broken china that was on the floor by her bed.'

There was a festival going on in the town. A band was playing in the market square, and all the pretty girls of Ober-weselberg – and some not so pretty ones, too – were dressed in their famous national costume, of flowery skirts, well-filled blouses and velvet waistcoats, and caps like cottage loaves. With sunshine faces and barley-sugar plaits, they bustled to and fro among the visitors, carrying trays of local cheese and Oberweselberg beer and wine.

'She no longer loves me! When her heart was changed, so was her mind!' thought Giorgio, with a pang of dismay, as he watched the pretty girls spilling over with foaming jugs and petticoats, while the band of the Oberweselberg Police popped and gurgled and bubbled like the local champagne. 'That's why she sent me down into the town to look for a bride for the veil! She was as good as telling me, "I am not for you!" Everything is lost!'

Suddenly the band stopped playing. Then, after a moment's pause, it burst forth, with a blaze of cornets and trombones, into the National Anthem.

35

The princess! God bless her and send her a worthy man! She stood in the middle of the market square, dressed just like the girls of Oberweselberg, as if she was no better than they. But of course she was so much more beautiful that, beside her, her rivals paled like candles before the sun.

Her eyes were wide and shining; and when they fell upon Giorgio, they sparkled and glittered as if with inward laughter and delight. Then she disappeared among her ladies-in-waiting; and the band played on.

Giorgio was overjoyed. Now he understood why she had told him to go down into the town. By being there herself, she was as good as telling him that *she* was the bride who was worthy of the veil! She still loved him. The change of heart had made no difference. If anything, thought Giorgio, it had improved her. The Serene Highness who had first greeted him had been lovely and radiant, to be sure; but that princess would never have come down into the market-place!

He left the town slowly, hoping for another glimpse of the princess. His head was full of agreeable sensations, and his face was a playground for smiles. Then he saw the old woman's cottage. It was standing fantastically on a grass island in the middle of a crossroads, where it had no right to be.

Instantly he was seized with terror! He bolted back to the castle as fast as his horse could carry him, rushed up to his room, locked the door, and collapsed on his bed.

The old woman had come for the golden heart! He was ruined, ruined! Unwillingly he stared at the wardrobe; still more unwillingly, he got up, opened it, and put his head inside. Very faintly he could hear the heart beating: thud – thud – thud! It sounded frightened. Or was it his own heart he was hearing?

Certainly he had good reason to be frightened. Was he not a mean and sneaking monster? Vainly he waited for a comforting, 'Na-ay!' but all he heard was the thud – thud – thud! of the stolen heart. He was alone with his crime.

Although . . . when you came to think about it . . . and put it in perspective (which meant pushing it a long way off), he hadn't actually committed the crime yet. The crime would only be when he gave the golden heart to the old woman. That's what had filled him with such horror. He hated the idea of it; which showed what a noble soul he had.

He went to the window and looked out across the ornamental gardens and down to tumble-roofed Oberweselberg, huddled beside the River Rhine. Even through his landlady's husband's field-glasses, he could see no sign of the old woman coming after him. Most likely she'd only come to Oberweselberg because, as she'd told him, she wanted to move to somewhere more convenient and nearer to the shops. She couldn't have known that he'd cut out the heart already.

He returned to the wardrobe and opened the black bag and took out the heart. He shuddered with the strange sensation its throbbing produced in him. He stared at it intently. What was its enormous value? Surely it was worth a good deal more than just its weight in gold; which, even at the current rate, would not amount to more than –

His calculations were interrupted by a knock on the door. Hurriedly he hid the heart and answered the door. A servant had come, carrying a splendid suit of clothes. It was the princess's wish that he should wear them. It seemed that Her Serene Highness had become wearied of seeing Signor Giorgio looking like a beggar at her table.

'She has never,' confided the servant with a puzzled smile, 'spoken like that before.'

'Because she has never loved before,' murmured Giorgio, when the servant had departed. 'I'll put back the golden heart tonight; and then I'll go.'

He had no choice. If he stayed, and married the princess, he'd have to give the old woman the golden heart. That was the bargain, and he could see no way round it. He was too honourable to try to cheat her; particularly as he was frightened of her and did not know what form her vengeance might take.

'So it's back to Padua, Giorgio, my friend,' he whispered sadly. 'Back to the dusty attic and the dusty philosophy. Unless – unless there's a secret in the golden heart that can save you . . .'

The poor student put on the fine clothes, and looked at the rich student in the mirror. He nodded. There was no doubt that wealth suited him better than poverty. The embroidered shirt and the long swallow-tail coat of green velvet the princess had sent gave him a gracefully serpentine look; which, with his black curly hair, his curving smile and his inkpot eyes, suddenly made you think of the Garden of Eden . . . Not that there was any connection between the upright Giorgio and Eve's serpent; except, of course, over the little matter of an apple.

At dinner, he received admiring glances all round; and the princess herself nodded approvingly, as if to say, 'If I am to be worthy of the veil, you must be worthy of me.' She herself was a wonderful sight; with diamonds at her breast and in her

39

hair, she sparkled and glittered as if she would outshine her own chandeliers.

Never before had she seemed so carefree and light-hearted; which was not to be wondered at, thought Giorgio, as the apple in her breast could not have weighed a quarter of what had been there before. She chattered away to those who sat nearest, and was continually provoking them into laughter with her wit . . . which she was kind enough to repeat more loudly for the benefit of those who might not have heard.

'I have never known you in such spirits, Your Highness,' remarked an elderly gentleman who was famous for his gravity.

'And I have never known *you* in any spirits,' returned the princess with a bright smile, 'Your Lowness!'

The poor man did not know where to look, and the laughter that greeted the princess's sally was more polite than warm. An uneasiness fell upon the table. People became cautious about what they said, for the princess seemed to have discovered an edge to her tongue, that could be wounding. It was a side to the princess that none had seen before; and, although outwardly she was as fresh and radiant as she'd ever been, it was felt that something different had awakened in her, and was stirring within . . .

It's love, thought Giorgio; and sighed.

'You look sad, Signor Giorgio,' said the princess suddenly. 'Do you not think,' she asked a lady-in-waiting, 'that our Signor Giorgio looks down in the dumps?'

The lady-in-waiting, a pretty young woman with black hair and green eyes, said, 'Yes, Your Highness.' Nobody could be sure which way this princess would jump, and if you didn't agree with her, it would probably be down your throat.

'Tell us, Signor Giorgio,' went on the princess to the student, 'did you not see the object of your quest in the town this morning?'

Giorgio sighed again; but did not answer.

The princess shrugged her shoulders impatiently, and turned back to the lady-in-waiting.

'We do not like to see sad faces at our table, do we?'

'Oh no, Your Highness,' answered the lady, with an eager smile.

'Sadness is so ugly, is it not?'

'Oh yes, Your Highness, indeed it is!'

'Even our Signor Giorgio looks ugly when he is sad, do you not think?'

'Oh yes, Your Highness!'

'Then you do not think he looks handsome?'

'Oh indeed I do, Your Highness! I have never seen anyone so handsome in all my life!'

'Handsome enough, shall we say,' pursued the princess, with a mysterious smile that made the lady-in-waiting feel exceedingly uncomfortable, 'to make anyone a desirable husband?'

'No doubt about it, Your Highness!'

'Would *you* marry him?'

The lady-in-waiting, not knowing whether the princess was serious or not, stuttered and stammered and grew very red in the face. Everybody was looking at her and waiting for her answer. She didn't know what to say for the best. If she said, no, the princess might be offended and come down on her like a ton of bricks. If she said, yes, everybody would be sure to laugh at her and a certain person, of whom she was very fond, would never speak to her again. Tears filled her pretty eyes and she gazed imploringly at Signor Giorgio for some present help in her need.

'I'm sure,' said Giorgio, gallantly coming to the rescue of beauty in distress, 'that so lovely a lady must already be promised elsewhere!'

The lady-in-waiting smiled at him so warmly and gratefully, that he could not help beaming with pleasure and pride. There really was no end to his good qualities!

'So, Signor Giorgio,' said the princess, who had not yet been promised elsewhere, 'you find my lady-in-waiting lovely?'

'All your ladies-in-waiting are lovely!' replied Giorgio, who liked to please everyone.

'Black hair and green eyes are very becoming, are they not?' said the golden princess, smiling her mysterious smile. 'Our Signor Giorgio is quite a judge of beauty.'

Soon afterwards she left the table, and everyone breathed a sigh of relief. Her mood had been so strange. Although her eyes had been bright, her colour high, and her manner lively, it was felt that there was something feverish and urgent going on inside.

'It's love,' reasoned the student of philosophy as he retired to his room with the buzz of worried voices still in his ears. 'It's the natural effects of love, and I am not to blame in the least; am I?'

He paused, and then said: 'Na-ay!' on behalf of his absent horse. He sat down heavily on his bed. He had drunk a simply tremendous amount of Oberweselberg wine, which had made him unsteady on his feet but wonderfully clear in the head. Which only went to show that the old philosophers were right when they'd said there was truth in wine.

For instance, he could now see quite clearly that he'd be a fool to throw away his chances with the princess on account of a bargain with a wicked, crazy old woman. After all, what could she do to him? Turn him into a frog, or something?

43

'Ha – ha!' laughed Giorgio ironically.

Nor, when you came to think about it sensibly, was there any need to put back the golden heart that night. In fact, it was quite out of the question. His hands weren't steady enough; and he was much too kind and good a person to risk harming the princess just because he liked to think of himself as a man of honour.

He nodded sagely. There was truth in wine, all right! You might almost have said that there was wine in truth, by the feeling of cheerfulness that each new thought imparted. It really was wonderful how everything suddenly seemed so plain and straightforward!

He stood up and tried to take off his coat, but lost his balance and fell heavily back on the bed. He lay still for a while, and then went to the window for some fresh air. He looked outside. A thin paring of the moon tarnished the quiet lakes and fountains of the ornamental gardens and turned Oberweselberg into a town of tiny silver.

'All mine!' mumbled Giorgio, kneeling down and resting his chin on the window-sill and beaming dazedly over the landscape. 'Two hundred rooms ... four hundred acres of unusual trees ... three breweries ... and – and a clear conscience ...'

Then he heard a scream! It was a horrible scream, sharp as a needle in the night. It was followed by another, and another. Then came a commotion of anxious voices and running feet.

The poor student turned grey with dread. He shuddered, and felt suddenly sick at heart. The best of the wine and the best of the truth dribbled away, and he was left with the worst: sickness and guilt. Although he did not want to know what had happened, he could not keep away. He left the room and crept downstairs, trembling in every limb.

There were hurrying candles and swirling dressing-gowns everywhere. Tousled footmen, and ladies-in-waiting, with butterfly curl-papers nesting all over their shrubbery heads,

44

hastened along the passages. Giorgio followed, trying to melt into nothingness, like an unhappy phantom.

But it wasn't the princess who had screamed. In fact, the disturbance hadn't even wakened her. To Giorgio's enormous relief, it turned out to have been a lady-in-waiting, the one with green eyes and black hair. Her room was bright with lights, and she herself was surrounded by eager comforters.

'A nightmare,' explained a servant to Giorgio. 'Poor lady! It must have been that roast lamb she had for supper.'

The poor lady lay back in a chair. She was as white as a ghost, and there was a scratch right across her face, from her eye to her chin.

'She must have done it herself,' confided the servant. 'Even nightmares don't make scratches like that.'

Her dream had indeed been terrifying. She'd fancied that she'd woken up to find a white-gowned figure bending over her and whispering:

'Green eyes, black hair! I must have them or I will die! Oh the pain, the pain! It's eating me up! Give me those eyes and stop the pain in my breast!'

Then fingers had reached out, and that's when she'd screamed and screamed, and the figure had vanished like a mist.

'There, there! It was only a nightmare, dear! You shouldn't have eaten roast lamb so late at night.'

The lady-in-waiting nodded and smiled feebly; and touched her cheek. She couldn't remember how or when she'd scratched herself; but that wasn't to be wondered at. She'd been frightened almost out of her wits as her dream had seemed so real. In fact, she must have struggled so wildly with her imaginary attacker that there were even spots of blood on the floor by her bed . . .

Curiously, Giorgio stared at them; and could not help noticing that they were not confined to the floor by the bed. Although they were very faint, having been trodden over by many feet, he could just make out that they led across the room and to the door.

Quietly he left the room. There was a spot of blood outside, in the passage. Then he saw another . . . and another . . . He followed them. His heart was beating furiously. The spots were close to the wall, as if someone had crept barefoot and secretly that way . . . someone whose foot had been cut and was still bleeding. At last the bloodstains stopped; and Giorgio found himself outside the door of the princess.

He knelt down and put his ear to the keyhole. Very faintly he heard the princess sighing and moaning in a strangely troubled sleep:

'Green eyes, black hair . . . I must tear them out to stop the pain . . . Oh the pain, the pain in my breast . . . Sharp little teeth . . . eating me, gnawing me . . . Oh!'

46

It had not been the roast lamb that had caused the lady-in-waiting to scream out in terror; it had been the princess!

Giorgio went back to his room. He was deeply troubled. Could what had happened really be due to the natural effects of love? Or was it because he, Giorgio of Padua, had made a mistake, a horrible mistake?

He sat down on his bed and clutched his head in his hands, as if it was in danger of flying off. He did not feel at all well. Nevertheless, if he had made a mistake (and he was prepared to admit that it was possible) then he must put it right. It was the only honourable thing to do.

He sat perfectly still, thinking hard; and listening. At last, the castle was quiet again, and wrapped in sleep. He stood up, and opened the wardrobe door. Then, taking what he needed, he went downstairs. He did not go directly to the princess's room, but to the castle's kitchens instead. There, after much searching in larders, poking about in pantries and peering inside covered dishes, he found what he was looking for. A heart. But this time, it was a heart far better suited to his purpose. He was a wiser student than he had been before; and, although his face was pale and his eyes were popping like corks, he knew what he was doing. There had been lamb for supper. What better then for the beautiful princess than the heart of that lamb? He wrapped it in muslin and hastened to the princess.

The perfume of roses had gone from her bedroom. In its place was a smell that was sickly sweet, and cloying. The princess was breathing evenly. She was fast asleep; but her sheets and pillows and coverlet bore testimony to dreams of a twisted, stormy and writhing nature. Her golden hair was all tangled, and her face, lit by the thin moon, glimmered with a feverish sweat; and it wore an ugly, gasping smile.

'A – a – a – ah!' she sighed, as her breast was laid open by the pale student's kingfisher shears, and the evil within was exposed.

The apple! It was half eaten away! In its midst, writhing and

47

twisting and nibbling and gnawing, there
wriggled a fat, unwholesome maggot!

'A – a – a – ah!' sighed the princess as the
rotting apple was plucked from her breast and
the heart of the lamb was put in its place.

Or – or had it been, 'Baa – aa – aah!' wondered
Giorgio, dazed by his own skill and daring?

Swiftly he sewed up the wound; and, when he had
finished, there was nothing to betray what he had
done, except for a single drop of blood that had fallen

on her coverlet, as before. The princess's face was calm, peaceful and innocent; and the student could have wept with relief.

'Ah Giorgio!' she murmured in her sleep, as he soothed her troubled hair and gently wiped the moisture from her brow.

'Heart of gold, heart of gold,
Must be given, never sold!'

THREE

Giorgio had another bad dream. He dreamed that the princess was dying, and only her golden heart could save her. But he couldn't open the wardrobe door! He tugged and tugged at it with all his might; but it was stuck fast. Then, suddenly, the door burst open; and, to his amazement and horror, out rushed an enormous torrent of blood!

He couldn't imagine where it was all coming from. It poured and splashed and tumbled everywhere. There was no stopping it. Already he could hear people downstairs, shouting and complaining that there was blood coming through the ceiling and running down the walls. The whole castle was bleeding.

People were banging on his door and calling to him. Frantically he hid under the bed-clothes to escape being blamed for all the blood.

'Signor Giorgio! Signor Giorgio!'

They were in his room. They were shaking him, furiously, violently!

'Signor Giorgio! Signor Giorgio! Wake up, wake up!'

He woke up. A servant was standing over him, smiling cheerfully. It was bright morning; and there was no blood anywhere.

'Her Serene Highness –' began the servant.

'How – how is the princess?' asked the student, wild-eyed from sleep and anxiety.

'Brisk and bonny as a lamb!' returned the servant fondly. 'She ate a hearty breakfast and went out directly. She had a strong desire, she said, to browse over the hillside, and to skip through the morning dew. God bless her!' he exclaimed warmly, and, with a deep, long look at Giorgio, added: 'And send her a worthy man!'

Then he went on to explain that Her Serene Highness had been graciously pleased to bestow upon Signor Giorgio another suit of clothes.

As the weather was fine, she desired that Signor Giorgio should be suitably dressed if he wished to enjoy the many beautiful and interesting walks about the castle. Accordingly, she had chosen for him the bristly jacket, hairy breeches, stout leather gaiters and the gaily feathered hat of an Oberweselberg country gentleman.

'Shall I hang the garments in the wardrobe, Signor Giorgio?' inquired the servant, his hand upon the fatal door.

'No! No!' cried out Giorgio, in sudden panic. 'I – I will get dressed directly!'

When the servant had gone, and his footsteps had died away, the student summoned up his courage and tried the wardrobe door. It was not stuck. He held his breath and opened it, inch by inch. Nothing worse came out than a large moth, grey as dust.

It made him jump. For a moment, he wondered if it could have been the old woman in disguise. Then he marvelled to have had such a foolish idea . . . although his professors in Padua would not have been surprised in the least. All his ideas were foolish, they thought.

Cautiously he poked his head into the musty darkness, and listened. He could hear the golden heart, softly thudding inside the black velvet bag. All was well. Dreams, he should have remembered, went by opposites, and held up the mirror only to fears. Mightily relieved, he shut the door, sat down on the bed, and took stock of his position.

Although his nightly studies had taught him that it was unwise to count your chickens before they were hatched, he saw no reason why he shouldn't count the eggs. His prospects, when you came to look at them sensibly, were as rosy as a summer's garden. The princess, far from dying, was as brisk and bonny as a lamb.

He couldn't help chuckling over how well his choice of a heart was turning out.

'God bless her and send her a worthy man!' the servant had said; and had given him such a look as made matters plain that everyone expected *him* to be that man. And why not? He sighed pleasurably as he thought how far he had come up in the world since his lonely nights in the dusty attic in Padua; and he wondered what his professors, who, one and all, had declared he would never amount to anything, would say if they could see him now.

'Ah Giorgio, Giorgio!' they'd cry. 'How wrong we all were!'

He put on his new clothes. They fitted perfectly, and he was amazed by how well the princess had taken his measure. He looked in the glass, and the poor student touched his hat to the sturdy country gentleman who stared proudly back. Once again, he felt that riches suited him far better than poverty.

He prepared to go out; then he recollected his horrible dream. He tried to dismiss it, but it wouldn't go away. A disagreeable thought struck him. If dreams went by opposites, what if his next dream should be a good one? He shuddered. He went back to the wardrobe, took out the throbbing velvet bag, put it inside his satchel, and slung it over his shoulder. All things considered, thought the student of philosophy, it was better to be safe than sorry.

> *'Heart of gold, heart of gold,*
> *Am I warm, or am I cold?'*

pondered Giorgio, brooding deeply over the heart's secret as he walked in green sunshine along a woodland path. He frowned and shook his head. 'Cold . . . cold . . .' he sighed, as the answer remained as mysterious as ever it had been.

He sat down upon a fallen tree-trunk, rested his chin on his fist, and stretched his brains till his eyes ached and his ears

buzzed. What was the answer? A thousand possibilities tempted him. Could it be like the gold that was supposed to lie at the bottom of the River Rhine, and would give its possessor power over all the world?

> 'Heart of gold, heart of gold,
> Am I warm, or am I cold?'

Cold . . . cold . . .

Was it, then, like those magic stones he'd read about, that gave whoever cast them the skill to read the future?

Cold . . . cold . . .

Maybe it was like the wonderful serpent's tongue that, people said, could wash out human ears and let them understand the language of animals and birds?

He listened. The woods were full of meaningless cheepings and chatterings. Cautiously he opened his satchel and took out the heart. He pressed it against his ear. Its uncanny warmth tingled like a million needles, and its throbbing sounded as loud as muffled hammers inside his head. Thud – thud – thud! and in between, he fancied he could hear a tiny murmuring and sighing, as if a small prisoner was pining to be free.

He took the heart away from his ear, and listened again to the chirpings and twitterings of the quarrelsome birds. He shut his eyes to sharpen his hearing . . .

'Pink – pink! Tsirrup – tsirrup! Tea – cher! Tea – cher!' he heard; and then, quite distinctly:

'Signor Giorgio! Signor Giorgio!'

Eagerly he opened his eyes. But it was no bird or wild woodland creature he had miraculously understood: it was the princess!

Guiltily, he hid the heart in his satchel and prayed with all his might that she hadn't seen it.

She was standing some dozen yards away, in dappled sunshine on the other side of the path: a princess of patches, green and gold. She came towards him, and the sunlight darted across her, like bright butterflies. She wore a gown of ivory silk, embroidered all over with a pattern of acorns and oak-leaves; and, as if to comfort the lamb's heart that beat in her breast, she wore widely flowing, leg-of-mutton sleeves.

Giorgio rose to his feet, doffed his hat and bowed. The princess nodded, and remarked on the manliness of his appearance, in particular on his fine head of hair which, she said, reminded her of a black fleece.

Giorgio beamed. Then the princess glanced down at the satchel that lay at the student's feet. Her eyes glittered with curiosity.

'What have you brought with you, Signor Giorgio?' she
asked. 'Something good to eat?'

Giorgio trembled; and his beaming changed to a paper smile
upon a paper face.

'No – no, Your Highness! N-nothing to eat, I assure you!'

She frowned; then she bent down and plucked a tuft of
grass, and nibbled at it in an absent-minded manner. Giorgio
saw that her slender fingers were thick with earth and grime;
and he wondered where the lamb had been straying . . .

The princess's eyes returned to the satchel.

'Have you,' she asked, 'brought the bride veil with you?'

'No, Your Highness.'

'Foolish, foolish! What if you had met a worthy bride here
in the woods? Did you not think of that, Signor Giorgio?'

'The – the thought never crossed my mind, Your Highness.'

'Why not? Was it frightened to get its feet wet?' she
demanded; and then laughed at the poor student's confusion.
'Tell me,' she went on abruptly, 'have you strong fingers and a
good nose, Signor Giorgio?'

The question startled him, but before he could think of anything to say, the princess shook her head impatiently.

'Never mind! I will find out for myself. Follow me, Signor Giorgio, follow me!'

Full of wonderment and curiosity, Giorgio picked up his satchel and followed the princess as she skipped and trotted briskly across the path and among the trees. She was very nimble in her movements, and Giorgio was hard put to keep up with her. From time to time she turned to look back and beckon him on with little grunts and cries of impatience.

'How strange,' thought Giorgio, 'for a lamb to be leading the way!'

'Signor Giorgio, Signor Giorgio! See what I have found!'

The princess, chuckling and squealing with delight, was on her hands and knees in the middle of a sunshine glade.

'Signor Giorgio –'

But Giorgio had no eyes for the kneeling princess. His bulging gaze was fixed elsewhere. His knees knocked, his brain tottered, and the blood congealed in his veins. On the edge of the glade, beside a scarlet speckled rose-bush, was the old woman's cottage on wheels!

'Signor Giorgio –'

There was no sign of the old woman or of the horse that must have drawn the caravan into the glade. He could see right into the crowded little sitting-room that he remembered so well. The old woman was not there.

'Signor *Giorgio*!'

The princess's voice had taken on a warmly pleading tone. Giorgio's blood began to stir once more through his veins; and thoughts, like frightened children, began to tiptoe through his brain.

The princess was smiling at him. And such a smile! There was no doubt that she loved him with all the gentle heart he had given her. His course was plain. He must take the final step and leave the golden heart in the old woman's cottage. Then he would be able to lead the princess like a lamb to the altar. The crime, taking everything into account, would only be a small one –

'Signor Giorgio!'

The princess's voice was in his very ear; and it was angry. She seized him by the shoulder and dragged him into the middle of the glade.

'Three times I called you!' she accused.

'But – but –'

'Goats butt, Signor Giorgio. And rams. Come now, my fine country gentleman! Let me see what a good nose you have, and what strong fingers!' She pointed to the earth at her feet, where she had already begun to scrape and dig with her fingers. 'Can you smell them, Signor Giorgio? I can; and they drive me wild with hunger! Dig, dig for me!'

She paid no heed to the cottage; it was as if her passion for what lay under the earth blinded her to everything else. She was down on her hands and knees again, sniffing and clawing . . .

'Dig, Signor Giorgio, dig, dig, dig, dig . . .'

Obediently he knelt beside her and began scraping at the earth; and he wondered uneasily what strange passion it was that her heart had inspired in her.

Suddenly his searching, thrusting fingers came upon a clump of warty black earth-nuts –

'Truffles!' squealed the princess; and, seizing them, stuffed them eagerly into her mouth! Greedily she chewed and chuckled, and black shreds hung from her lips, as if she was eating spiders.

Terrified, he tried to stop her, for he feared that she would poison herself. She snarled and grunted, and turned upon him savagely.

'Keep away from me while I am eating!'

He stared at her in horror and amazement. What had he done, what had he done?

She scrabbled in the earth for more truffles; but, finding none, crawled upon her hands and knees to the edge of the glade, where the ground was soft and muddy. Then, calling for him to join her, she began to roll and wallow in the filth!

Helplessly the poor student watched as the beautiful princess, shrieking with pleasure, writhed and twisted in the slime. The sight was horrible; and the fouler she became, the wilder grew her delight.

'What have I done, what have I done?' whispered Giorgio, as the oozy, slimy princess, worn out by her frantic wallowings, fell into a snoring sleep.

He stared down at the foolish, filthy, greedy grin that disfigured her lovely face, and tears came into his eyes.

He knew too well what he had done. In the darkness of the

kitchen, he had taken, not the heart of a gentle lamb, but the wild and brutish heart of a pig!

'Your Highness,' he murmured, kneeling down beside her. 'Your Serene Highness –'

She made no answer. She was fathoms deep in swinish slumber. He looked back towards the cottage, half-expecting to see the old woman in her armchair, grinning at him, and holding out her skinny hand for the golden heart. But the cottage was quiet, and no one else was in the glade.

How fortunate, he thought, how very fortunate it was that he had not taken the final step and committed the crime. There was still time to undo what he had done. But he must be quick . . .

Carefully he wiped away the mud and filth from the princess's breast. She grunted, but did not awaken. He opened his satchel and took out the leather case containing the scissors and the needle and thread. Then he took out the black velvet bag.

'Ah Giorgio!' he sighed. 'If only you had had another day! Surely you would have discovered the secret, and the world would have been yours.'

He looked again towards the cottage, and his gaze fell upon the rose-bush that grew beside it. The red blossoms spotted the green like a shower of blood. Their perfume filled the glade; they were wonderfully beautiful . . .

'No, Giorgio!' muttered the poor student, as he felt temptation rise within him once more. 'Have you not already made two most terrible mistakes?'

He opened the velvet bag and took out the golden heart. Sunlight flashed upon it as it lay, beating, in his hand, like all the treasure of the earth.

'One more day, Giorgio, just one more day!' he pleaded with himself.

'No, no!' he warned sternly. 'Remember your mistakes!'

'Oh I do – I do!'

He nodded vigorously. Then he frowned. Of course he had made mistakes. It was only to be expected. If nothing else, his nightly studies had taught him that the man who never made a mistake never made anything. It was the only way to learn. In fact, when you came to think about it properly, the more mistakes you made, the wiser you would be. It was no good at all, thought the student of philosophy, being right first time.

He put back the golden heart in the velvet bag and tiptoed to the rose-bush. Shrewdly he examined the scarlet flowers. Which should he choose? One by one, he studied them, searching for the little worms and cruel insects that could bring disaster, and for the cankered petal that might bring a strange malady. At last he fixed upon one perfect bloom, and plucked it from the bush.

'This time,' he breathed, as he cunningly removed the thorns, 'this time you have thought of everything!'

'A – a – a – ah!' sighed the princess, as the red rose was laid in her opened breast.

> *'Heart of gold, heart of gold,*
> *Must be given, never sold.'*

He buried the pig's heart in the hole that had been dug for truffles, and carefully covered it over. Once more there was nothing to betray what he had done, save for a single drop of blood that had fallen on the bodice of the princess's gown.

FOUR

The princess was deeply ashamed to see how foul and muddy she was. She couldn't understand how she had come to fall asleep and lie in the mire 'like a pig', she said; and blushed to the colour of her heart.

She thanked Signor Giorgio warmly for having awakened her and, taking his arm, began to walk back towards the castle.

'A little slower, Signor Giorgio,' she begged. 'We are not being pursued, you know.'

Giorgio begged Her Highness's pardon and moderated his pace, which had indeed been brisk. In fact, his gaitered legs had been going like a pair of scissors in his haste to get away from the cottage before the old woman came back and caught him.

They strolled gently, the bristly country gentleman and the soiled princess; and every moment they loitered was agony to the poor student. It's tempting Fate, he thought; and could only hope and pray that Fate was a more honourable person than he, and would not be so easily tempted.

'I love the sun!' murmured the princess, as a golden beam fell aslant her, like the gorgeous sash of some Grand Order.

As she lingered, a bee rose up from a wayside flower, a bumble-bee that hummed and buzzed and fidgeted round her head. Anxiously Giorgio tried to wave it away with his hat. The bee danced and dodged, bobbed and curtsied, and settled, like a brown velvet button, on the bodice of the princess's gown.

'It *knows!*' thought Giorgio, as the insect began to fumble at the princess's breast. 'It knows what's inside!'

She looked down, and exclaimed in alarm. The bee flew up, alighted for a moment on Giorgio, then hummed away in a puzzled zigzag among the trees, as if eager to spread amazing murmurs in the hive.

★

Giorgio dreamed; and this time his dream was a good one. He dreamed that he had discovered the secret of the golden heart, and it turned out to have been so simple that he could have laughed aloud at his own blindness in not having seen it before.

It was, to be sure, a fine secret, and it filled him with a glorious sensation of sunshine. He had a strong feeling of having brought great happiness to all the world; and his professors in Padua came to him with tears in their eyes, and heaped heartfelt thanks upon his head.

'No, no!' he protested modestly. 'It was only —'

And then he woke up and couldn't, for the life of him, remember what he had been going to say. And worst of all, he couldn't remember the secret. It had been whisked out of his mind's reach like the hem of a bright gown, vanishing. He could have wept with bitter disappointment! The secret had been within his grasp; and now it was lost again.

'Signor Giorgio, Signor Giorgio!' came the servant's morning voice, following on the morning knock upon the door. 'Her Serene Highness,' he went on, coming into the room with a swoop and a glide, and drawing back the curtains to let the sunshine in, 'bids Signor Giorgio good morning and hopes that he slept well.'

'Indeed I did,' said Giorgio, rubbing his dazzled eyes. 'And – and Her Highness . . .?'

'Like an angel,' returned the servant, laying a suit of clothes over the back of a chair. 'As if she was folded up in night, she said. God bless her and send her a worthy man!'

What had the princess chosen for him this time? Giorgio wondered, climbing out of bed when the servant had gone. He scratched his head. The clothes were carefully wrapped in white linen, as if to keep them fresh and clean. Something delicate and summery, he supposed; perhaps, even, he thought with a wry smile, something with a richly embroidered buttonhole . . .?

He looked. The princess had sent a swallow-tail coat, knee-breeches, courtly shoes, and a silk cravat. They might have been the garments for a royal wedding, except for one thing. They were all black, lustreless, undertaker's black.

He puzzled over the princess's choice, but could make nothing of it. He dressed himself and looked in the mirror. He shivered slightly. Although the clothes suited him wonderfully well, his sombre appearance struck a chill into his heart. Then he thought of his good dream and felt cheerful again.

He left the room and, after breakfast, went outside into the gardens to join the princess in the sun. His heart was light and his hopes were high as he hastened across the smooth green lawns with his swallow-tails flapping, black as his shadow's brother.

The princess was lovely beyond compare; but the student of philosophy had learned to look more deeply than that. She was fragrant, fond and tender in her feelings; but he had learned to look more deeply even than that. She was, as the saying goes, a rose without a thorn; and that was as deeply as Giorgio could look, try as he might.

Nevertheless he watched her carefully; he listened to her every tone of voice. He observed the way she dressed, he noted the way she walked, and he paid the closest attention to her smiles and eyes. Never in his life before had he studied with such zeal. Had he devoted himself to his books with half the care he lavished on the princess, he would have been wiser than all his professors in Padua University put together. He had no time, even, to puzzle over the secret of the golden heart; the princess herself filled his every thought. He dared not be wrong again . . .

She loved the sun, and would sit in it for hours at a time, while Giorgio stood behind her, holding a parasol to shield her from burning.

'God bless our Princess Charlotte!' people said. 'At last she has found a worthy man!'

She loved weddings and, in particular, brides. She would

attend even the humblest ceremony in Oberweselberg; and everybody longed only for the day when she herself would be the bride.

Most of all Giorgio longed for it; and often, as he stood behind her, he wondered if the time was ripe for him to kneel and offer her the enchanted veil. Several times he made the attempt; but on each occasion the words stuck in his throat.

'Your Highness –,' he would begin, in a voice that trembled in spite of himself.

She would turn, and look at him; and he would catch his breath and look away. Her eyes would be brimming with tears; and he would feel as sombre as when he'd first put on his swallow-tail black.

Why did she weep, and why had she sent him black? These questions puzzled him mightily, and he could not help wondering if, despite all his care, there had been some invisible sickness in the rose.

But the days went by in peace and beauty, and the princess smiled as often as she sighed. She was in good health, thought Giorgio: he had not been wrong.

'Your Highness,' he murmured, one sunshine morning, as he and his shadow hovered on the green. He had summoned up his courage, and he held the bride veil in his hand. 'Your Highness –'

She turned and gazed up at him with tear-bright eyes.

'Ah Signor Giorgio, Signor Giorgio!' she sighed, and sadly shook her head. 'The summer's almost done,' she said. 'Soon the swallows must fly.'

The student faltered and bowed his head. He had felt a sudden pain. It was as if in his own breast there lay, not a rose without a thorn, but a thorn without a rose, so sharp had been the prick and so dull and barren the ache it left behind. At last he knew why the princess wept, and why she had sent him black.

'Her Highness looked a little pale this evening,' went the word round the dinner-table after the princess had retired for the night. 'Don't you think so, Signor Giorgio?'

'No, no!' answered the student, struggling vainly against the truth. 'It was only the light!'

'Her Highness seemed a little tired this morning,' said the servant who came to awaken him. 'Though her room was warm, Signor Giorgio, she felt quite chilled, she said.'

'No, no!' cried Giorgio. 'It must have been cold in the night!'

But as the days went by the princess grew paler and paler,

and could not stop shivering, even in the sun. Her cheeks seemed crumpled, and the tears in her eyes were as forlorn as dew on a withering flower.

The princess was dying, and Giorgio knew it. With the coming of autumn the rose in her breast was fading away.

'Tomorrow,' she whispered, as she walked and stumbled, leaning upon Giorgio's arm and resting her tired head against his shoulder, 'tomorrow, Signor Giorgio, the swallows must fly and find another summer. Alas! mine has gone.'

It was three o'clock in the morning. The castle was fast asleep, save only for the poor student of philosophy. Dreams both good and bad fled from him, as if there was a face inside his head that frightened them. Wearily he rose from his bed and opened the wardrobe door. He put on his old clothes and, taking his heavy satchel, crept from the room.

He went down the stairs to the floor below. He turned left and drifted, like a ghost, along a passage until he came to a corner. He had the strangest feeling that his life was going backwards. He turned right and crept along to the end. He reached the door with the crown above it. He paused, but only for a moment; and then went into the princess's room. His cheeks were wet with tears.

Her bed floated in moonlight, like a pale ship upon a silver sea. He listened. The room was deathly quiet, and the smell of roses was almost sickly. He drew near and stood, looking down. The princess was as white as her pillow; her lovely features were as faint as a faded sketch. She scarcely breathed. Quickly the student knelt and opened his satchel . . .

'A – a – a – ah!' sighed the princess, as her golden heart, with its secret as mysterious as ever, was put back in her breast.

> 'Heart of gold, heart of gold,
> Has been given, has been sold . . .'

Silently, Giorgio left the room. This time he had been so skilful that not even a drop of blood had fallen to betray what he had done. All that remained on the princess's coverlet was the crumpled petal of a dying rose.

'God bless you, Princess Charlotte,' whispered the poor student, as he departed sadly, leaving his hopes behind. 'And – and send you a worthy man!'

FIVE

'My old professors were right after all,' sighed Giorgio, as he led his horse cautiously out of the castle's stables. 'I'll never amount to anything, don't you think!'

He waited; but the creature was too well-fed and sleepy to reply.

'Come, now,' he went on, 'we must find the old woman and give her back her terrible gifts.'

They went up into the dark woods and searched every path and moonlit glade.

'Mother, mother!' called Giorgio softly. 'I want to give you back your gifts. I was not the man you took me for; I am going back to Padua, to my dusty attic and books.'

But the woods were quiet and the glades were empty; the cottage had gone.

'Perhaps she has gone back to the town,' thought Giorgio, mounting his horse, for it was downhill all the way, 'to be nearer running water and the shops.'

But the quaint old streets of Oberweselberg were deserted, and none but cats crossed the cobbled square. The old woman and her queer cottage were not in the town.

Giorgio went down to the River Rhine and stood upon the quayside, where the steamers called, twice a day. He stared down into the restless water, beneath which, it was said, mysterious maidens ,dwelt and played. He opened his satchel and took out the leather case and the black velvet bag.

'Take them!' he cried, to whatever women lived under the

70

Rhine. 'Maybe you can find a better use for magical scissors, needle and thread!'

Then with all his strength he hurled them into the middle of the river.

It was almost dawn when he left the town, and mid-morning when he was back among the leafy by-ways and lanes. Everything had been green when he'd come; now everything was golden brown, and leaves, not butterflies, fluttered in the air.

The sun was bright, but there was not much warmth, either in the morning or in Giorgio's heart. He wished he'd kept the old woman's needle and thread to mend his flapping, draughty sleeve.

'At least,' he said to his old companion, in an effort to comfort himself, 'I never really committed the crime. In the end, I always did up what I had undone. Don't you think so?'

'Na-ay!' answered the horse, with a mighty shake of its head.

'But I gave her back the golden heart!' protested Giorgio. 'Surely that was enough?'

'Na-ay!'

'Then what more could I give?' wept Giorgio, quite at the end of his tether. 'My life?'

'NA-AY!' shrieked his horse, rearing up in alarm as they rounded a bend in the road. 'NA-AY! NA-AY!'

There was something in the way! Giorgio's eyes grew huge. He clutched at his horse for support. His heart gave one enormous thump and then, so far as he could tell, stopped altogether.

Beside the road, just as it had been before, was the old woman's battered armchair!

But it was not the old woman who was calmly sitting in it, dressed in brown velvet and plaiting her golden hair as if to while away the time. It was the princess!

But it couldn't be! At any moment she'd turn into the malignant old woman and demand the return of her scissors, her needle and thread!

'And when she finds out I haven't got them,' thought the poor student of philosophy, miserably, 'she'll turn me into a frog!' He peered fearfully among the trees for a glimpse of the terrible cottage; but he saw only the princess's horse, solemnly banqueting off grass.

'I knew you must come this way, Signor Giorgio,' said the sudden princess, unfolding her hair and shaking her head into a little storm of gold. 'So when I found out that you'd gone, I rode like the wind to catch you.'

She stood up and her velvet sighed and flowed. 'You left this behind you,' she said; and held out the marvellous bride veil.

She paused, as if waiting for Giorgio to say something. He held his tongue. The princess began to look uncomfortable, and to fidget with her dress. Giorgio could not help noticing that it had been flung on in haste over her night-gown, which kept spilling out, like milk. She blushed when she saw him looking at it.

'You must not think, Signor Giorgio,' she said, with

something of a princess's pride, 'that I have come galloping in pursuit of *you*. I mean, for you alone. It was because of the veil . . . and – and your quest. My heart, you know, was touched.'

She knows! thought Giorgio in terror. She knows! He waited for the horror and loathing and contempt that would surely be turned upon him. But they did not come.

'You do believe me?' said the princess anxiously. 'You do believe that I came only to give you back the veil?'

'Yes, yes! Oh yes, Your Highness!'

'Then you are a fool, Signor Giorgio!' cried the princess in exasperation, and very much as his professors had done. 'Even your horse has more sense than you!'

Giorgio looked and saw that his old companion had wandered off among the trees and joined the princess's mare. Their heads were close together as they contentedly munched the grass.

'Oh Giorgio, Giorgio!' sighed the princess, as if suddenly wearied with a student who would not learn. 'Do you not know that I love you?'

'Why?' asked Giorgio, taken by surprise. 'Why?'

'Why?' repeated the princess. 'How can I know why? Perhaps it's because of your great dark eyes and black curly hair? Perhaps it's because of your smile? Perhaps it's because you are two inches taller than I, and are kind to your horse? Or perhaps it's only because I wanted to be worthy of the veil? But one thing I can promise you, Signor Giorgio, it's not because of your deep learning in philosophy! I love you, Signor Giorgio, and you must be content with that. Surely your nightly studies must have taught you that when we look for reasons, we have ceased to love.'

She held out the veil; and Giorgio, scarcely knowing what he did, took it from her and laid it about her shoulders, where it clung like a mist.

'I did not want,' he said, 'to hide your face.'

'Ah Giorgio!' she sighed. 'Come, let's ride home together!'

★

74

They rode slowly, side by side; bending low under overhanging branches, and coming out into sunshine, surprised and crowned with leaves.

'Do you love me, Signor Giorgio?' the princess thought to inquire, as they drew near to Oberweselberg-on-the-Rhine. 'I only ask because you have never told me that you do.'

'I love you dearly,' returned Giorgio. 'I love you with all my heart.'

'Why?'

'How can I know that?' said Giorgio, who could learn well enough when he chose to. 'Perhaps it's because of your golden hair, perhaps it's because of your fine blue eyes? Perhaps it's because of the way you walk, or perhaps it's because of the way you smile? Perhaps it's because of your ornamental gardens, your woods and your many unusual trees?'

'And what of my breweries and my two hundred rooms?' put in the princess, as if anxious that she should not be undervalued. 'And my trade on the River Rhine?'

'Perhaps,' nodded Giorgio gravely. 'Perhaps.'

'And what of my heart of gold?' pursued the princess, with a look that was strange and mysterious. 'Did you not think of that?'

She knows, thought Giorgio, and this time without fear. She knows. He looked at her, but she was now gazing serenely ahead. So they rode on together, and Giorgio wondered and wondered about his princess.

He wondered if she'd guessed from the tell-tale drops of blood, and the petal of the withered rose? He wondered if the old woman had told her; and sometimes he wondered if, in some strange way, she and the old woman were one?

But it didn't matter. They knew the worst and the best of each other; and what remained was the truth of love, which was the middle ground.

'Heart of gold, heart of gold,' whispered Giorgio, thinking once more of the great treasure he had put back in his princess's breast.

'Has been given, has been sold,' she murmured; and at last he knew the secret of the golden heart.

He smiled. He had known it in words all the time; but it was only now that he knew what it meant. It was the one treasure in all the world that increased with the spending; and he felt rich beyond compare.

'Your poor sleeve!' exclaimed the princess, as they rode into the town. 'When we get home I will mend it for you!'

They were married at the end of September in St Wesel's Cathedral. There was, needless to say, tremendous rejoicing, and dancing in the streets. The fountain in the town square flowed, not with beer, but with the very best local champagne; and the band of the Oberweselberg Police played polkas and waltzes, while petticoats foamed like beer.

Foreign royalty graced the wedding, and among the many guests was a party of professors from Padua University, in striped trousers, tail-coats and top hats.

'We always knew,' they said to their student, with happy tears in their eyes, 'that you'd make something of yourself, Giorgio, my boy! We always knew that you'd fall,' they chuckled, 'on your feet!'